ODDS AND EVENS

A NUMBERS BOOK

ODDS
and EVENS

by Heidi Goennel

TAMBOURINE BOOKS
NEW YORK

Library of Congress Cataloging in Publication Data

Goennel, Heidi. Odds and evens: A numbers book/Heidi Goennel. p. cm.
Summary: Counts to thirteen in terms such as one-horse
town, six of one, eight ball, and baker's dozen.
1. Counting—Juvenile literature. [1. Counting.] I. Title.
QA113.G64 1994 513.2'11— dc20 [E] 93-15420 CIP AC
ISBN 0 - 688 -12918 - 8. — ISBN 0 - 688 -12919 - 6 (lib.)
1 3 5 7 9 10 8 6 4 2
First edition

To Peter

1 · 2 · 3 · 4 · 5 · 6 · 7

A one-horse town

8 · 9 · 10 · 11 · 12 · 13

1 • 2 • 3 • 4 • 5 • 6 • 7

Two in the bush

8 • 9 • 10 • 11 • 12 • 13

1 • 2 • 3 • 4 • 5 • 6 • 7

Three blind mice

8 • 9 • 10 • 11 • 12 • 13

1 · 2 · 3 · 4 · 5 · 6 · 7

A four-leaf clover

8 · 9 · 10 · 11 · 12 · 13

1 • 2 • 3 • 4 • 5 • 6 • 7

The five senses

8 • 9 • 10 • 11 • 12 • 13

1 · 2 · 3 · 4 · 5 · 6 · 7

Six of one and half-a-dozen of the other

8 · 9 · 10 · 11 · 12 · 13

1 • 2 • 3 • 4 • 5 • 6 • 7

Seventh heaven

8 • 9 • 10 • 11 • 12 • 13

1 • 2 • 3 • 4 • 5 • 6 • 7

Behind the eight ball

8 • 9 • 10 • 11 • 12 • 13

1 • 2 • 3 • 4 • 5 • 6 • 7

A cat has nine lives

8 • 9 • 10 • 11 • 12 • 13

1 • 2 • 3 • 4 • 5 • 6 • 7

Ten-gallon hat

8 • 9 • 10 • 11 • 12 • 13

1 • 2 • 3 • 4 • 5 • 6 • 7

The eleventh hour

8 • 9 • 10 • 11 • 12 • 13

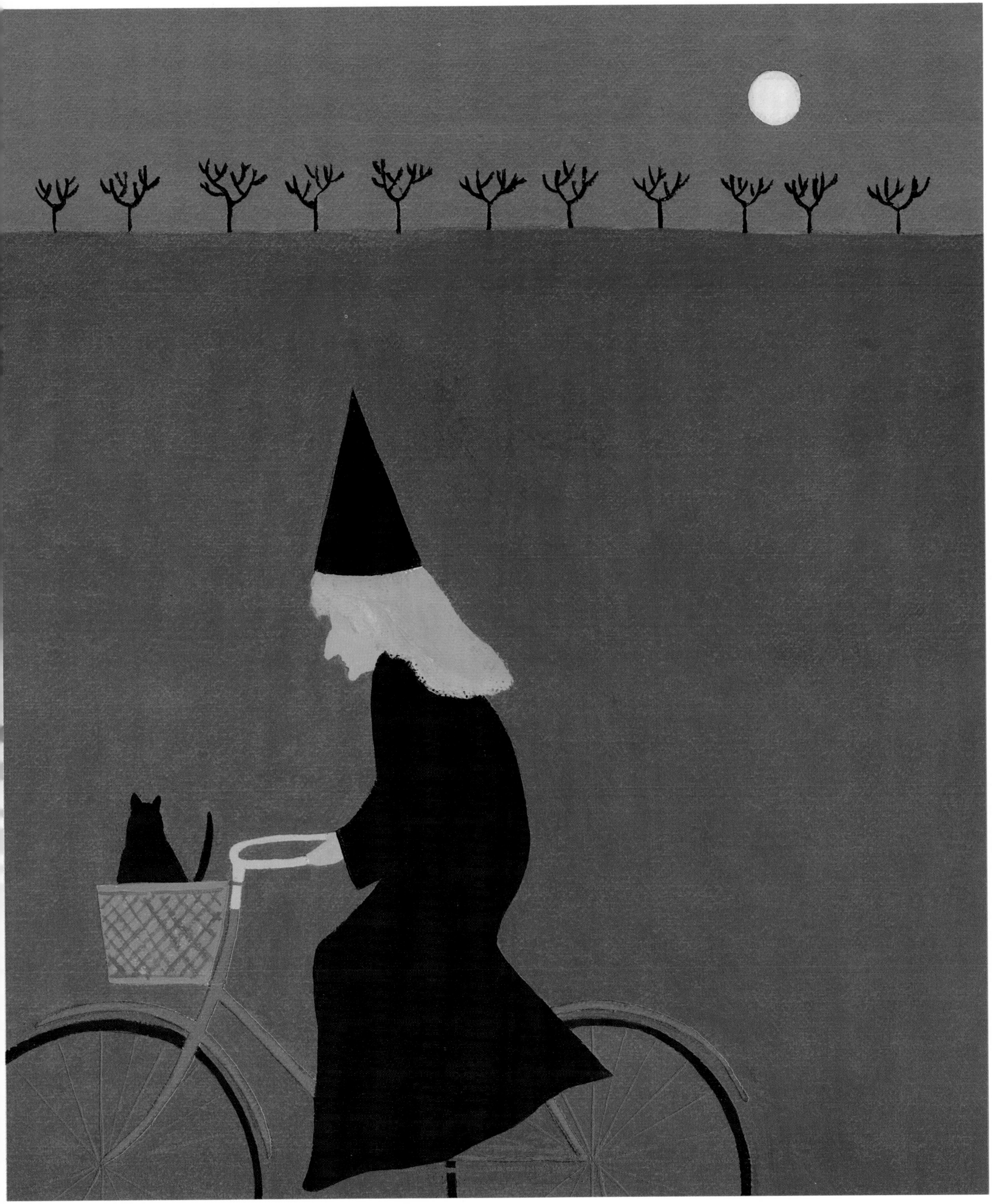

1 • 2 • 3 • 4 • 5 • 6 • 7

The clock strikes twelve

8 • 9 • 10 • 11 • 12 • 13

1 • 2 • 3 • 4 • 5 • 6 • 7

A baker's dozen

8 • 9 • 10 • 11 • 12 • 13

1 · 2 · 3 · 4 · 5 · 6 · 7

8 · 9 · 10 · 11 · 12 · 13